AFRICAN AMERICANS IN SPORTS

JAMES NASIUM

TITLES IN THIS SERIES

AFRICAN AMERICANS IN SPORTS

JAMES NASIUM

MASON CREST
PHILADELPHIA

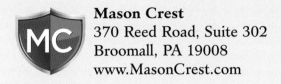

Mason Crest
370 Reed Road, Suite 302
Broomall, PA 19008
www.MasonCrest.com

Copyright © 2013 by Mason Crest, an imprint of National Highlights, Inc.

Printed and bound in the United States of America.

CPSIA Compliance Information: Batch #MBC2012-11. For further information, contact Mason Crest at 1-866-MCP-Book.

First printing
1 3 5 7 9 8 6 4 2

Library of Congress Cataloging-in-Publication Data

James Nasium, 1961-
African Americans in sports / James Nasium.
    p. cm. — (Major Black contributions from emancipation to civil rights)
Includes bibliographical references and index.
ISBN 978-1-4222-2381-9 (hc)
ISBN 978-1-4222-2394-9 (pb)
1. African American athletes—History—Juvenile literature. 2. Sports—United States—History—Juvenile literature. I. Title.
GV583.M335 2012
796.0896'073—dc23

                            2011051950

Picture credits: Associated Press: 39; Brown University News Service: 22; Getty Images: 51; Harvard University Archives: 20; Library of Congress: 8, 11, 14, 16, 17, 18, 26-27, 29, 31, 33, 34, 36, 46, 47; Phil Anthony / Shutterstock.com: 54; Featureflash / Shutterstock.com: 52; Ffooter / Shutterstock.com: 13; FlashStudio / Shutterstock.com: 3; photogolfer / Shutterstock.com: 7; Dmitry Yashkin / Shutterstock.com: 55; Official White House Photo: 41, 44.

TABLE OF CONTENTS

INTRODUCTION

Dr. Marc Lamont Hill

It is impossible to tell the story of America without telling the story of Black Americans. From the struggle to end slavery, all the way to the election of the first Black president, the Black experience has been a window into America's own movement toward becoming a "more perfect union." Through the tragedies and triumphs of Blacks in America, we gain a more full understanding of our collective history and a richer appreciation of our collective journey. This book series, MAJOR BLACK CONTRIBUTIONS FROM EMANCIPATION TO CIVIL RIGHTS, spotlights that journey by showing the many ways that Black Americans have been a central part of our nation's development.

In this series, we are reminded that Blacks were not merely objects of history, swept up in the winds of social and political inevitability. Rather, since the end of legal slavery, Black men and women have actively fought for their own rights and freedoms. It is through their courageous efforts (along with the efforts of allies of all races) that Blacks are able to enjoy ever increasing levels of inclusion in American democracy. Through this series, we learn the names and stories of some of the most important contributors to our democracy.

But this series goes far beyond the story of slavery to freedom. The books in this series also demonstrate the various contributions of Black Americans to the nation's social, cultural, technological, and intellectual growth. While these books provide new and deeper insights into the lives and stories of familiar figures like Martin Luther King, Michael Jordan, and Oprah Winfrey, they also introduce readers to the contributions of countless heroes who have often been pushed to the margins of history. In reading this series, we are able to see that Blacks have been key contributors across every field of human endeavor.

Although this is a series about Black Americans, it is important and necessary reading for everyone. While readers of color will find enormous purpose and pride in uncovering the history of their ancestors, these books should also create similar sentiments among readers of all races and ethnicities. By understanding the rich and deep history of Blacks, a group often ignored or marginalized in history, we are reminded that everyone has a story. Everyone has a contribution. Everyone matters.

The insights of these books are necessary for creating deeper, richer, and more inclusive classrooms. More importantly, they remind us of the power and possibility of individuals of all races, places, and traditions. Such insights not only allow us to understand the past, but to create a more beautiful future.

In 1947, Jackie Robinson became the first African American to play in baseball's major leagues during the 20th century. His accomplishment opened the way for greater participation and acceptance of black athletes in other sports.

SMASHING BASEBALL'S COLOR BARRIER

On Tuesday, April 15, 1947, more than 26,000 fans filled Ebbets Field in Brooklyn, New York. They were there to watch the Brooklyn Dodgers open their season against the Boston Braves. Brooklyn had a new player in its lineup wearing number 42. As he jogged across the grass that afternoon to take his position at first base, Jackie Robinson made history. The 28 year old became the first African American to play major league baseball in the 20th century.

Robinson's presence on the baseball field ended a 59-year-old ban on African-American players in professional baseball's highest league. His success opened the way for other blacks in baseball, as well as other sports. Robinson also inspired black Americans off the field. He gave them hope that someday they might have the same rights as whites.

In the 1940s, many white Americans didn't want blacks and whites to mix. They wanted to keep African Americans separate, or segregated. In some states, particularly in the South, blacks could not eat in the same restaurants as whites. They couldn't drink from the same water fountains. Black children were not allowed to attend the same public schools as white children. Blacks could not even use the same hospitals as whites.

"We believe that [Robinson's breaking the color barrier] was the beginning of the modern-day Civil Rights movement in our country," explained Bob Kendrick, a historian and president of the Negro Leagues Baseball Museum. "When you put it all together, you have a story that is actually bigger than the game of baseball itself."

During the 1947 season, Robinson repeatedly faced racial hatred both on and off the field. Many fans and players didn't want this grandson of slaves in the major leagues. Some players spat at him. Pitchers threw balls at him. Fans called him ugly names. Some people even sent him death threats. "We have already got rid of several like you," one note said.

Robinson didn't respond. Before the season, he had promised Branch Rickey, the general manager of the Brooklyn Dodgers, that he would not fight back. "The taunts angered him, sometimes frightened him, but he turned away from them," his wife Rachel Robinson later said. Robinson understood that if he fought back, it could be used as an excuse to keep other black ballplayers out of the major leagues.

DAZZLING FANS

Jackie Robinson was probably not the best African-American baseball player in the United States when Branch Rickey signed him to a contract in 1945. Other players like home-run hitter Josh Gibson or pitcher Satchel Paige had more career accomplishments. But Rickey thought that Robinson had the right combination of talent and temperament to succeed.

Jackie Robinson had been born on January 31, 1919. His family were poor farmers in Georgia, but the Robinsons eventually moved to Pasadena, California. Jackie wasn't the only athlete in the family. His older brother Mack was a runner who won a silver medal at the 1936 Olympic Games,

behind only Jesse Owens. In high school, Jackie was a varsity athlete for the baseball, basketball, football, and track teams. He then went to college at the University of California in Los Angeles (UCLA), where he again competed in baseball, basketball, football, and track.

In 1943, soon after the United States entered World War II, Robinson was drafted into the military. He became a second lieutenant and was assigned to the 761st Tank Battalion. However, he never saw combat.

After the war ended, Robinson agreed to play baseball for a Negro League team, the Kansas City Monarchs. He was a shortstop on the team during the 1945 season. He played well enough to attract the attention of Branch Rickey. The Dodgers' general manager decided that Robinson was smart, talented, a family man, and had "the guts not to fight back" against racial hatred.

On October 23, 1945, Robinson signed his historic contract with the Dodgers. "Of course, I can't begin to tell you how happy I am that I am the first member of my race in organized baseball," he told reporters that day. "I realize how much it means to me, to my race and to baseball. I can only say I will do my very best to come through in every manner."

In the 1946 season, Robinson played for the all-white Montreal Royals, Brooklyn's minor league team. He ended the year with a .349 batting average and scored 113 runs. He helped his team win the minor league championship.

Jackie Robinson in his Kansas City Monarchs uniform, 1945. In 47 games that season, he hit .387 with five home runs and 13 stolen bases.

TRAIL-BLAZING MOVE

In April 1947, Robinson made the trail-blazing move to the major leagues. He later said of his first game, "I was nervous in the first play of my first game at Ebbets Field, but nothing has bothered me since." The Dodgers defeated Boston, 5-3, with Robinson scoring the go-ahead run in the eighth inning.

Jackie Robinson faced taunts and threats, but in time he won the country's approval. His speed and electrifying base running dazzled fans and other players. In his first year with Brooklyn, Robinson stole 29 bases. He had a .297 batting average and won the National League Rookie of the Year Award. "[Robinson] had all the attributes to handle the racial hatred he would have to deal with," said Bob Kendrick. "Jackie had the mental tough-

"He's My Friend"

In his first game away from Brooklyn's Ebbets Field, Jackie Robinson faced a tough crowd. The Dodgers were playing in Cincinnati, and the Reds fans were yelling racial slurs. They wanted to scare and anger the young ballplayer. Even the Reds' players were taunting him from the dugout.

Brooklyn's team captain was Harold "Pee Wee" Reese. The white short-stop was liked and respected by nearly everyone in the league. As the taunting continued, Reese walked over to first base. He put his arm around Robinson's shoulder and spoke with him.

"[Reese] stared into the Cincinnati dugout and said, 'Hey, he's my friend. It says Brooklyn on my uniform and Brooklyn on his and I respect him," Robinson's teammate, pitcher Ralph Branca, later recalled.

The stadium fell silent. Reese's action had squelched the yelling. Robinson and Reese would become good friends. They played together in Brooklyn until Robinson retired after the 1956 season.

ness. He was married and had stability in his life. He had served in the military and was already a celebrated athlete because of his time at UCLA."

During his third season, Robinson stole a career-best 37 bases and ended the year with a .342 batting average. He was named the Most Valuable Player (MVP) in the National League that year.

Robinson played in the major leagues for 10 seasons, all of them with the Dodgers. He helped the Dodgers win their first World Series in 1955. After the 1956 season, Robinson retired. During his career, Robinson scored 947 runs, earned a .311 batting average, and he stole 197 bases. When Jackie Robinson retired from baseball in 1956, almost every major league team had at least one black player.

After he left baseball, Robinson became a businessman and civil rights leader. He died on October 24, 1972, of a heart attack at the age of 53.

Baseball has continued to honor his legacy. In 1962, Robinson became the first African American elected to the Baseball Hall of Fame. Baseball's Rookie of the Year Award is now called the Jackie Robinson Award. And every major league team has retired his number 42.

This memorial to Jackie Robinson is part of a special display on the ballplayer inside the baseball stadium of the New York Mets.

Heavyweight champion Jack Johnson was the most famous African-American athlete of the early 20th century.

2

EARLY AFRICAN-AMERICAN SPORTS HEROES

Fifteen three-year-old horses trot onto a dirt track. The sound of their hooves echoes through the crisp air. The ground rumbles under their weight. A young colt named Aristides, wearing a green blanket with an orange stripe, tosses its head. The jockey on its back—a 19-year-old African American named Oliver Lewis—guides the chestnut colt to the starting line.

A hush comes over the crowd at the Louisville Jockey Club. It's 2:30 P.M. on May 17, 1875. A drum beats. A flag drops. In a blur of dirt and dust, the young horses take off. Aristides pulls ahead for an early lead on the one-and-a-half mile course. With four horses in hot pursuit, Aristides runs strongly. Lewis guides the colt through the home stretch. Aristides crosses the finish line two lengths ahead of the next horse.

Lewis may not have realized it at the time, but he had just galloped into horse racing history. The black jockey had won the first Kentucky Derby. Today, this is one of the oldest and most prestigious horse races held in the United States.

Lewis won that historic race just 12 years after President Abraham Lincoln had signed the Emancipation Proclamation. This document declared that millions of African-American slaves would be freed as of January 1, 1863. However, most slaves did not become free until the end of the Civil War in 1865. The Thirteenth Amendment to the U.S. Constitution, ratified in 1865, officially abolished slavery.

Despite these national laws, in the years that followed African Americans didn't have the same freedoms as whites. They didn't have the same rights. And they weren't on the same playing fields—even in sports.

"American sports are filled with records of African-American athletes capable of participating in the broad sports arena but not given the chance due to their race," writes Professor Melvin R. Sylvester of Long Island University. "As sports grew into an American popular pastime, it also grew along on separate fields with race as a dividing line."

The 1901 Kentucky Derby was won by Jimmy Winkfield (1882–1974), a black jockey who also won the 1902 race. Winkfield remains the last African American to win the prestigious Derby. With his opportunities to ride in the U.S. blocked due to racism and segregation, Winkfield moved to Europe in 1904. There, he was able to enjoy a lucrative and successful racing career.

One of the greatest jockeys in American history was Isaac Murphy (1861–1896). He was the first jockey to win the Kentucky Derby three times, in 1884, 1890, and 1891. During his career the African-American rider won an amazing 44 percent of his races—a record that no jockey, black or white, has ever equalled. Murphy was the first jockey elected to the National Museum of Racing and Hall of Fame when it opened in Saratoga Springs, New York, in the mid-1950s.

Some black athletes rose above those dividing lines. African-American jockeys, like Oliver Lewis, made some of the earliest strides. Many black jockeys were former slaves who had groomed, trained, and raced horses for their white owners. Thirteen of the 15 riders in the first Kentucky Derby were African Americans. Black jockeys won 15 of the first 28 Derby races. Black horsemen trained five of the winners between 1875 and 1902.

By the early 20th century horse racing was becoming more popular. This meant more white jockeys looking for work, resulting in fewer opportunities for blacks to ride. Also, throughout the country segregation of blacks and whites became more common, especially in the southern states. Segregation meant that soon black jockeys found themselves unable to ride on the nation's top racetracks. Between 1903 and 1921, just two African-American jockeys competed in the Kentucky Derby. After 1921, no black jockey would ride in the race for nearly 80 years.

CRACKING BARRIERS IN SPORTS

Pioneering black athletes made their marks in other sports that were popular in the late 19th century and early 20th century. In addition to horse racing, these included baseball, football, and boxing. No matter the sport, things were never easy for black athletes.

Baseball started being played before the Civil War, but the sport's pop-

ularity grew after the 1860s. By 1867 there were more than 400 baseball clubs. Some of these teams included both black and white players. Most teams included only black players, or only white players. Most of the players were amateurs, meaning they weren't paid to play.

In the 1870s, professional baseball leagues began to form. The National League began play in 1876 with eight teams based in large cities. The teams paid their players, and charged admission to see the games. Today

African-American baseball players from Morris Brown College in Atlanta, circa 1899.

the National League is one of two leagues known as the "major leagues." The other is the American League, founded in 1901. These leagues are considered to have the best professional players. There were other baseball leagues where the players were paid to play, but because the teams were located in smaller cities and the players were not as good, they were known as the "minor leagues."

> **— Did You Know? —**
> In 1871, the first organized baseball game between a black team and a white team took place in Chicago. The black Uniques faced the white Alerts. The Uniques won, 17–16.

At the same time that professional baseball was developing into a popular spectator sport, changes in American society meant fewer opportunities for African-American baseball players. The Thirteenth, Fourteenth, and Fifteenth Amendments to the U.S. Constitution had freed the slaves and given African Americans the same rights as white citizens. However, during the 1870s many states, particularly in the South, began to pass laws that restricted the rights of blacks. Often, blacks were kept separate, or segregated, from whites.

Baseball teams across the country became divided by race. Some whites refused to play on, or against, teams that had black players in the lineups. And some states didn't let black players on the same fields as whites.

THE FIRST BLACK PROFESSIONALS

In 1878, a baseball player named John "Bud" Fowler (1858–1913) became the first African American to play for a professional team. He pitched for a minor league club called Lynn Live Oaks in the International Association. Fowler played professional baseball for 10 seasons. He never reached the major leagues, although he did play in some exhibition games against major league teams.

Many people believe Moses Fleetwood Walker (1856–1924) was the first black player in major league baseball. Walker started his professional baseball career in 1883 with a minor league team, the Toledo Blue

Stockings of the Northwestern League. A year later, the team joined a major league of the 1880s, the American Association. Walker, a catcher, played 42 games with the Blue Stockings in the 1884 season before being injured. His brother, Weldy Walker (1860–1937), also played for the Blue Stockings during the 1884 season.

After recovering from his injury, Moses Walker played five more seasons in the minor leagues. However, by 1890 the white owners of teams in all of the professional baseball leagues, major and minor, had agreed not to hire black ballplayers for their teams. That decision kept African Americans out of major and minor league baseball for nearly 60 years.

BLACK PLAYERS IN FOOTBALL

Another sport that became popular in America during the late 19th century was football. The rules for the modern game of football were developed during the 1860s and 1870s. Colleges began to field football teams, and by the 1890s small towns all over the United States would have teams of amateurs that would play against the football squads from other nearby towns.

For most African Americans, their best chance to play football, especially in the South, was provided by all-black colleges. In 1892, Biddle College defeated Livingston College in what is considered the first black college football game.

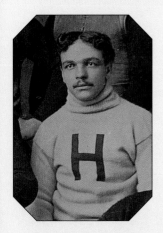

William Henry Lewis

Only a handful of African Americans had the chance to play at predominantly white colleges in the North. One was William Henry Lewis (1868–1949), who in 1892 became the first black football player named to the All-American team. He earned that honor the following year, too. Lewis played center for Amherst College and Harvard University, and later coached football at Harvard for 12 years. He was considered an expert on football, and even wrote a book about the rules.

Lewis graduated from Harvard's law school, and worked as a lawyer while coaching football. In 1910 he was appointed a U.S. Assistant Attorney General. This

is a high-ranking position in the federal government, and made Lewis one of the top legal officers in the country. He was the first African American appointed to this position.

Other black players who starred at white colleges included William T. Jackson, a running back who played with William Lewis at Amherst in 1889 and 1890, and William A. Johnson, a running back at the Massachusetts Institute of Technology in 1890. George Jewitt (1870–1908) became the first African-American to play at the University of Michigan, where he starred as a running back and kicker in 1890 and 1892.

Between 1889 and 1920, more than 50 African Americans played on white college teams. However, there were rarely more than two blacks on any team, and most colleges had no black players at all.

BLACKS IN PRO FOOTBALL

As in baseball, professional football leagues began to be organized as the sport became more popular. In the 1890s, some local teams began to pay players, and by the early 1900s professional football leagues were being formed. As in baseball, the legalized segregation of the time carried over to football, and few blacks were offered opportunities to play professionally.

One who did get a chance to play was Charles Follis (1879–1910), who signed a contract with the Shelby Athletic Club in Ohio as a running back in 1902. He was nicknamed the "Black Cyclone" because he was a fast runner who was hard to tackle. However, his pro career only lasted three seasons, in part because white players on opposing teams tried to hurt him on the field. He was also subjected to taunting and racial slurs from other fans. Follis was a great athlete who also played professional baseball for an all-black team.

Between 1902 and 1919 there were several pro football leagues. In 1919 a new organization, the the American Professional Football Association (APFA), was created. The APFA would eventually become the National Football League, the premiere pro football league.

During the 1920s and 1930s, the pro teams did not attract as many fans

as college football teams did. Owners of the pro teams often hired college stars in order to generate interest and boost attendance. This provided an opportunity for a few black players. One of them was Frederick Douglass

Fritz Pollard

"Fritz" Pollard (1894–1986), who had starred as a running back for Brown University. In 1916 he had become the first African American to play in the Rose Bowl, and was named to the All-American team that year. In 1919, a team called the Akron Pros signed him to a contract. The Akron Pros joined the APFA in 1920, and Pollard continued to play on the team through 1921. In the 1921 season, he took over as head coach. He is considered the first black NFL head coach.

Pollard played for several teams between 1922 and 1926. Wherever he played, he often faced racial hatred. Some fans threw bottles and rocks at him when he walked on the field. Fritz Pollard was elected to the Pro Football Hall of Fame in 2005.

Another black NFL player was Robert "Bobby" Marshall (1880–1958). He played for three different teams between 1920 and 1924. He and Fritz Pollard are considered the first African Americans to play in the NFL.

After the 1926 season, there were no black players on NFL teams. In 1933, the NFL team owners agreed not to hire black football players. That ban would last for more than a dozen years.

KNOCKOUTS

Like horse racing, boxing was a sport that African Americans often participated in before the Civil War. The white plantation owners would arrange boxing matches between their slaves and bet on the outcome. There were no timed rounds, so the matches often lasted until one of the fighters could no longer stand. There were few rules, either—the fighters could kick, throw, and choke their opponents. They fought without gloves. It was a

brutal sport. Many states had laws against boxing, but the fights were held anyway.

In the mid-1860s, formal rules for boxing matches were established by a British nobleman, the Marquess of Queensberry. His rules divided boxers into weight classes (lightweight, middleweight, and heavyweight), established three-minute-long rounds, with a one-minute break between them, and required boxers to use gloves. After this, boxing gradually became a popular organized sport, with most of the best fighters coming from the United States and the United Kingdom.

During the late 19th century, African Americans were permitted to fight in the lightweight and middleweight classes. However, they were generally not allowed to fight for the heavyweight championship. This was considered the most prestigious title in boxing. The greatest heavyweight champions of the time, including John L. Sullivan and Jim Jeffries, refused to fight black boxers.

Joe Gans (1874–1910) was the first black boxer to win a world title. On May 12, 1902, he won the world lightweight championship when he beat Frank Erne. Gans threw a right-handed knockout punch in the first round to claim the title.

Gans held the lightweight champion title from 1902 to 1908. During his career, Gans fought 171 professional fights. He won 145 of those duels—100 with knockout blows—lost 10 and tied 16. He was famous for his speed, agility, power, and ring savvy.

JACK JOHNSON

The first African American to win a heavyweight title was John "Jack" Johnson (1878–1946). Born in Galveston, Texas, Johnson began boxing when he was about 18. Over the next 14 years he won many fights against both black and white boxers. However, he could not get a shot at the heavyweight title. Finally, in December 1908, the heavyweight champion Tommy Burns agreed to fight Jack Johnson in Australia. The fight lasted 14 rounds before the fight was stopped and Johnson declared the winner.

White boxing fans were angry and upset, with many calling for a "great

white hope" to defeat Johnson in the ring. In 1910 undefeated former champion Jim Jeffries decided to come out of retirement to fight Johnson. The fight was called the "Battle of the Century," and was held in Reno, Nevada. Jeffries had not only never lost, he had never even been knocked down. Most people thought he would win the heavyweight title back. However, Jeffries was old and out of shape, and Johnson knocked him out in the 15th round.

Over the next five years, Johnson defended his heavyweight title many times. However, the "color bar" against black fighters remained in place. Johnson only defended his title against white fighters, and didn't give other top African-American boxers like Jeremiah "Joe" Jeannette (1879–1958) and Sam Langford (1883–1956) a shot at the title. Both of those boxers held the title of "colored heavyweight champion" at different times.

Jack Johnson was extremely controversial because of his behavior outside the ring. He had white girlfriends, and eventually married three different white women. He was a proud public figure, and was not afraid to taunt and insult whites. His victories in the ring made him wealthy, and he did not hesitate to flaunt his wealth. At a time when African Americans were expected to act humble and deferential to whites in public, his behavior shocked and offended many white Americans. On the other hand, blacks considered him a hero for standing up to racism.

Jack Johnson lost the heavyweight title to Jess Willard in a fight in Cuba on April 5, 1915. Today, Jack Johnson is considered one of the greatest heavyweight fighters of all time.

3

LEAGUES OF THEIR OWN

On February 13, 1920, a former baseball pitcher and team manager named Andrew "Rube" Foster led a private meeting of eight men in an old YMCA building in Kansas City, Missouri, They had one goal. They wanted to form their own baseball league. It would be a league like no other in the 1920s. All the players would be professional. They would be the best in baseball. And they would be African Americans.

Why did the men at the meeting want to start their own league for black players? They had no choice. Black baseball players in the 1920s couldn't join white professional teams. "Rube knew that if Negroes were to play in a professional league, we'd have to organize it ourselves," author Kadir Nelson wrote in *We Are the Ship*, a history of the Negro Leagues.

NEGRO NATIONAL LEAGUE FORMS

When the baseball team owners left that building in 1920, they had formed the Negro National League. It had eight teams: the Kansas City Monarchs, the Cuban Stars, the Detroit Stars, the American Giants, the Chicago Giants, the St. Louis Stars, the Indianapolis ABC's, and the Dayton Marcos.

Members of the Kansas City Monarchs and the Hilldale Baseball Club pose in front of grandstands filled with spectators before the first game of the 1924 Colored World Series.

Other black baseball leagues soon formed across the country. The American Negro League, Eastern Colored League, and Negro Southern League had all started by 1926. They played in Canada, Mexico, Cuba, and Latin American countries, too.

Negro League teams barnstormed across the country, playing teams of any race in small towns. The teams weren't always well organized, though. They didn't have much money. Some teams didn't have matching uniforms.

But Negro League teams pumped money and jobs into black communities. They also brought the best African American players in baseball—men and women—to local ballparks.

In October of 1924, the two top teams in the Negro Leagues played the first "Colored World Series." The matchup pitted the Kansas City Monarchs against an eastern team called Hilldale Club. Kansas City won the 10-game series. The popularity of Negro League baseball kept growing. The teams in the Negro Leagues did well for the next five years.

Unfortunately, the good times ended after October 1929, when the stock market crashed. The United States was soon plunged into a period of economic hard times known as the Great Depression. Many businesses closed, and millions of people lost their jobs. Without money, many fans stopped going to baseball games. Both white and black teams suffered. The

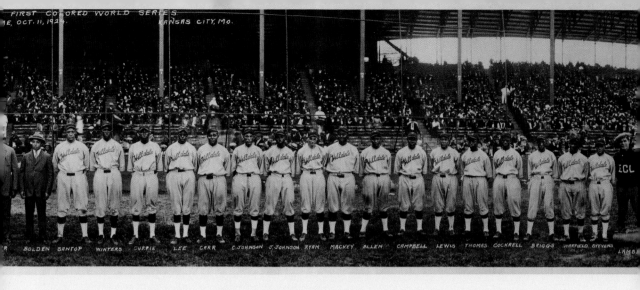

Negro National League soon collapsed. The American Negro League and the Eastern Colored League disappeared, too.

THE NEW NEGRO NATIONAL LEAGUE

By 1933, William "Gus" Greenlee helped build a new Negro National League. Greenlee owned one of the teams in that league: the Pittsburgh Crawfords. A slugger named Josh Gibson was one of its stars. He earned the nickname "the black Babe Ruth" because of his power at the plate. During his 17-year-career in baseball, Gibson smashed more than 800 home runs. His lifetime batting average in the Negro leagues was .354.

In 1937, teams in the Midwest and the South formed the Negro American League.

But the Negro National League folded in 1948. Teams in the Negro American League stopped playing in 1960.

Why did these leagues disappear? Baseball historians say Jackie Robinson's breaking of the color barrier in 1947 was a big reason. After Brooklyn signed Robinson, other major

> **═ Did You Know? ═**
>
> More than 2,600 men and women played in the Negro leagues during its history, according to Gregory Backer, president of the Negro Leagues Baseball Museum.

league teams began to hire black ballplayers. The fans followed the best players and stopped going to Negro League games.

ALL-BLACK BASKETBALL LEAGUES

The game of basketball was invented in the early 1890s by James A. Naismith, a gym teacher in Springfield, Massachusetts. The game was fun, and soon it was being played all over the country.

Pioneering Women in Baseball

The Negro leagues opened doors for hundreds of young black men who wanted to play professional baseball. It opened those same doors for black women. In the 1950s, three pioneering women joined the league.

Toni Stone was the first woman in the Negro leagues. She signed with the Indianapolis Clowns in 1953. She was 22. The second baseman played 50 games with the Clowns and had a .243 batting average. Indianapolis traded Stone to the Kansas City Monarchs in 1954. She played for Kansas City one year. Stone died on November 2, 1996. She was 65.

Indianapolis signed another female ball player to replace Stone. Right-hander Connie Morgan was 19 when she joined the Clowns. Morgan played second base during the 1954 and 1955 seasons. She died on October 14, 1996. She was 61.

Mamie "Peanut" Johnson also played in the Negro leagues. She joined the Clowns in 1953. She was 22. Johnson was a right-handed pitcher. She had a 33-8 record with the Clowns.

Johnson and the other women in the league barnstormed across the country with their teams. They shared the field with some of the greatest players in the Negro leagues. Many were gentlemen, but a few were disrespectful to the women players—at least until they recognized that the women were good ballplayers. "After you strike three or four of them out and, you know, it's alright," recalled Johnson.

Because of the segregation laws and policies of the time, African Americans were often not allowed to play on basketball teams with white players. Instead, they played on all-black teams. By 1908, a number of all-black basketball teams had formed an amateur league, called the Olympian Athletic League. That year, a team from Brooklyn called the Smart Set Athletic Club won the title of the first "Colored Basketball World Champion." Other top teams had names like the Monticello Delany Rifles and the Loendi Big Five. The Loendi Big Five won the Colored Basketball World Champion title four straight years, from 1920 through 1923.

By the early 1920s, professional all-black teams began to form. The first of these was the Commonwealth Five, founded in 1922. Another team, the New York Renaissance (or "Rens"), was founded in 1923. They barnstormed across the country like baseball teams in the Negro Leagues. The Rens played more than 100 games a year, often against teams of white players. Their toughest rivals were a team called the Original Celtics, the dominant white team of the 1920s and 1930s. When the first tournament for professional basketball teams (the World Professional Basketball Tournament) was held in 1939, the Rens beat an all-white team to win the championship.

A counselor teaches basketball to African-American girls in Montgomery, Alabama, during the 1930s.

In 1927, a new all-black professional basketball team called the Savoy Big Five was formed. The team later changed its name to the Harlem Globetrotters. The Globetrotters were one of the best of the pro teams that barnstormed the country during the 1930s. They won the World Professional Basketball Tournament in 1940. The team later became known for its fancy passing, slick ball-handling, and comic antics on the court.

OVERCOMING OLYMPIC HURDLES

In track and field, two female black athletes had a shot at Olympic gold during the 1930s. Sprinters Louise Stokes (1913–1978) and Tidye Pickett (1914–1986) qualified for the 1932 Olympic Games, which were held in Los Angeles. They were the first African-American women to earn spots on the U.S. Olympic team. However, although they had qualified for the team, they did not get to compete. The U.S. Olympic Committee pulled them off their relay team. They claimed that the two white women who replaced them were faster—even though Stokes and Pickett had beaten both of them when they qualified for the Olympic team.

Stokes and Pickett also qualified for the 1936 Olympics. The Olympic Committee again pulled Stokes from her event. She watched from the stands, disappointed, as the U.S. 4x100 relay team won gold. But Pickett ran the 80-meter hurdle race. Although she was disqualified in the semifinals, Pickett became the first African-American woman to compete on a U.S. team in the Olympic Games.

JESSE OWENS

Pickett accomplishment was overshadowed by the performance of black sprinter Jesse Owens, who won four gold medals at the 1936 Olympic Games in Berlin, Germany. He became the first U.S. athlete to win that many medals in a single Olympics.

Owens had been born in 1913 in Alabama. In 1920, his family moved north to Cleveland, Ohio. They were part of a general movement by

Early African-American Olympians

Jesse Owens was not the first African-American to compete for the U.S. Olympic team. At the 1904 Olympics in St. Louis, Missouri, runner George Poage (1880–1962) took home the bronze in the 200-meter and 400-meter hurdles. That same year, another athlete named Joe Stadler (born 1887; death date unknown) won silver in the standing high jump. He also won the bronze medal for the standing triple jump event.

John Baxter Taylor (1882–1908) became the first African American to win an Olympic gold medal. He was a member of the 1600-meter relay team that sprinted to victory in the 1908 Olympics in England. Tragically, Taylor died suddenly just five months after the Olympic Games.

William DeHart Hubbard (1903–1976) was the first African American to earn a gold medal for an individual performance in the Olympic Games. In the 1924 Olympics at Antwerp, Belgium, he won the long jump.

In this photograph of President Teddy Roosevelt with the 1908 U.S. Olympic Team, John Baxter Taylor is pictured in the back row, center, to the left of the president.

African Americans out of the South between 1910 and 1940 known as the Great Migration. Blacks moved north to major cities, hoping to find better jobs and less discrimination. When he was in high school, Owens showed incredible talent as a sprinter and long jumper. He was permitted to enroll at Ohio State University, where he won national championships in the 100 yard dash, 220 yard dash, 220 yard hurdles, and long jump in both 1935 and 1936.

Despite this success, Owens had to deal with discrimination. He was not allowed to live in the same dormitory on campus as the other athletes. When the track team traveled, he was not allowed to stay in hotels with his white teammates or eat in the same restaurants as whites.

In 1936 Jesse Owens was selected for the U.S. Olympic team, and traveled to Berlin for the Olympic Games. At that time the Nazi Party of Adolf Hitler ruled Germany. Hitler and other Nazi leaders believed that white Germans—whom they called "Aryans"—were superior to all other races. Blacks, along with Jews and others, were considered inferior, or not as good as Aryans. Hitler had said that victories by German athletes in the Olympic Games would show the world that Germans truly were the superior "master race."

Owens singlehandedly proved that Hitler's theories were wrong. He won both the 100 and 200 meter sprints, the long jump, and was a member of the American 4x100 relay team. Hitler was so angry that he left the Olympic stadium without shaking Owens's hand.

Many Americans, both white and black, were happy that Jesse Owens had shown up Hitler and the Nazis. However, his four Olympic gold medals did not change the attitudes of millions of white Americans, who believed they were better than blacks. "When I came back to my native country, after all the stories about Hitler, I couldn't ride in the front of the bus," Owens later recalled. "I had to go to the back door. I couldn't live where I wanted. I wasn't invited to shake hands with Hitler, but I wasn't invited to the White House to shake hands with the president, either."

After the 1936 Olympics Owens was unable to cash in on his athletic fame. He worked at several different jobs. Jesse Owens died in 1980.

Jesse Owens competes in the 200 meter sprint at the 1936 Olympic Games in Berlin.

BOXING CHAMPION JOE LOUIS

The year after Jesse Owens's record-breaking Olympic performance, another African American named Joe Louis fought his way into history. In 1937 Louis became the second black boxer to win the World Heavyweight title. "The Brown Bomber" won that honor when he knocked out James Braddock during an eight-round match.

Louis had been born in Alabama in 1914, and when he was a teenager his family had been part of the Great Migration, moving north to Detroit. He began boxing to earn extra money at the start of the Great Depression in the early 1930s. As Joe Louis became a rising star in the heavyweight boxing division, his agent and trainer were careful about the way he was portrayed in the media. They did not want him to be controversial and flamboyant like Jack Johnson had been. Louis gained a reputation as a fair fighter who was modest and clean-living. This helped make him popular among both black and white boxing fans, and enabled him to get a shot at the heavyweight title.

When Louis won that title, not everyone was ready to call him the champion. Braddock had arranged to fight Louis in 1937 instead of the boxer who was supposed to be next in line for a heavyweight title fight.

Heavyweight champ Joe Louis in training for a fight at Greenwood Lake, New York, 1941.

That boxer, a German named Max Schmeling, had shocked the boxing world in 1936 when he beat Louis in 12 rounds. It was the first time Joe Louis had ever lost a fight. Louis would need to beat Schmeling to prove that he deserved the heavyweight title.

The rematch, held on June 22, 1938, was considered one of the major sporting events of the year. German leader Adolf Hitler had claimed that Schmeling's previous victory supported Nazi racial theories. Just as Jesse Owens had in 1936, Louis would prove those theories to be silly. The African-American prizefighter knocked out Schmeling in the first round. The fight made Joe Louis a national hero.

For the next 11 years, Louis defended the heavyweight title. He won 25 straight matches as champion, a record for heavyweights, and retired still holding the title in 1949. Joe Louis died on April 12, 1981, at the age of 66. Ten years later, he was elected to the International Boxing Hall of Fame. Many people consider him the greatest heavyweight boxer of all time.

Althea Gibson stretches for a ball during the 1957 Wimbledon tennis tournament. That year Gibson became the first African American to win the prestigious event.

4

BREAKING BARRIERS

A crowd packed Cleveland's Municipal Stadium. More than 60,000 fans filled the stands on September 6, 1946. The Cleveland Browns faced the Miami Seahawks. This was a big game. It was the Browns' first game ever. And the team was playing in a new professional football league—the All-American Football Conference (AAFC).

Something bigger happened on the field that night that changed the face of professional football. Two African Americans suited up in Browns' uniforms for that season opener. They were middle guard Bill Willis and fullback Marion Motley. They became the first black players in the AAFC. They also permanently broke the color barrier in professional football. And the Browns won the game, 44–0.

Professional football at that time had an unwritten ban on black players. The teams and leagues denied there was such a rule. But they weren't signing the top black football players in college. No African Americans had played in the established professional league, the NFL, since 1933. The Browns bucked that rule. Head coach Paul Brown vowed to sign the best players, regardless of color.

Two other black football players also appeared on pro football rosters in 1946. The Los Angeles Rams, a new team in the NFL, signed defensive end Woody Strode and running back Kenny Washington, who were teammates from the University of California Los Angeles (UCLA). Their signing marked the end of the color barrier in the NFL.

The NFL's Greatest Running Back

Jim Brown is often called the greatest football player ever. The list of records this Hall of Fame running back set on the gridiron could fill a playbook.

Born in Georgia in 1936, Brown moved to Long Island, New York, when he was eight. He emerged as a football star in high school, then attended Syracuse University, where he was an All-American running back. The NFL's Cleveland Browns picked him in the first round of the 1957 draft.

Brown played nine seasons for Cleveland and never missed a single game. In eight of those seasons, Brown led the NFL in rushing. For his career, Brown gained a total of 12,312 yards. He scored 126 touchdowns. Brown earned the league's Most Valuable Player (MVP) award four times.

In the 1965 season, Brown was at the top of his game. He led the league in rushing with 1,544 yards, and in touchdowns with 17. He was only 29 years old. But before the 1966 season Brown shocked the sports world by retiring. He wanted to be an actor.

Brown made it big on the silver screen. He starred in more than 50 movies, including *The Dirty Dozen* and *100 Rifles*. He also appeared on TV shows like *The A-Team*.

In 1971, Brown was elected to the Pro Football Hall of Fame. "Jim Brown was a superb craftsman whose primary job was to run with the football for the Cleveland Browns," the Hall of Fame says of Brown. "For nine seasons, he did it better than any player before him."

This 1952 photo of veteran Cleveland Browns players includes running back Marion Motley (#36) and defensive lineman Bill Willis (#60).

Other football teams soon added black players to their rosters. In 1949, the Chicago Bears became the first team in the National Football League to draft a black player. The Bears picked George Taliaferro in the 13th round. But the halfback from Indiana signed with the Los Angeles Dons, a team in the rival AAFC. In 1953, Willie Thrower became the first black quarterback in the NFL. He played for the Chicago Bears.

The AAFC stopped operating after the 1949 season and some of the teams, including the Cleveland Browns, joined the NFL. Both Marion Motley and Bill Willis were still with the team, and they helped the Browns

win the NFL championship in 1950. Motley led the league in yards by a running back, and Willis was chosen for the Pro Bowl as one of the league's best defensive players. After their playing days were over, both Motley and Willis were elected to the Pro Football Hall of Fame.

SLOW OFF THE DRIBBLE

Basketball was a little slower to progress. The Basketball Association of America—the forerunner of the modern National Basketball Association (NBA) started in 1946. But at first team owners didn't hire black players.

A player named Don Barksdale helped to change attitudes. In 1948, Barksdale became the first black player on the U.S. Olympic basketball team. Barksdale was a 6-foot-6-inch forward and center who had played college basketball at UCLA. During the 1948 Olympic Games in London, he scored 54 points in seven games. The United States beat France, 65–21, to win the gold medal.

Three players can say they were the "first" African Americans in the NBA. On April 25, 1950, Chuck Cooper became the first black player drafted by an NBA team. The Boston Celtics picked him in the second round. Cooper was a 6-foot-4-inch power forward. He played in the NBA for six seasons.

Another player named Nat "Sweetwater" Clifton became the first black player to sign a contract with an NBA team. Clifton played his first game as a New York Knick on November 3, 1950. The 6-foot-7-inch forward played in the NBA for eight seasons and averaged 10 points a game.

But the first African American to actually appear in an NBA game was Earl Lloyd. He made his first NBA court appearance with the Washington Capitols on October 31, 1950. The former star at West Virginia State University played nine seasons in the NBA.

Don Barksdale also received an opportunity to play in the NBA. In 1951 he signed a contract with the Baltimore Bullets. He played two seasons for that team, and in 1953 he became the first black player named to the all-star team. He was traded to the Boston Celtics later that year, and continued playing until 1955. In 2012, Don Barksdale was elected to

Vice President Joe Biden greets Earl Lloyd (right), the first African American to play in an NBA game, during Lloyd's 2010 visit to the White House. Lloyd played nine seasons in the NBA, scoring more than 4,300 points. His best season came in 1954–55, when he averaged 10.2 points and 7.7 rebounds per game and helped the Syracuse Nationals win the NBA championship.

the Naismith Memorial Basketball Hall of Fame in Springfield, Massachusetts.

INTEGRATING TENNIS AND GOLF

In the first half of the 20th century, most Americans did not play sports like tennis and golf. These were regarded as sports for wealthy people. Many people, both black and white, could not afford the lessons or equipment needed to play golf and tennis well. There were few golf courses or tennis courts open to the public. Most were owned by country clubs, which refused to admit non-white members.

In the 1950s and 1960s, Althea Gibson helped to open doors for black athletes. Gibson was a great tennis player. When she was growing up, she had participated in a recreational tennis program in Harlem, New York. She showed such talent that she was encouraged to join the Harlem Cosmopolitan Tennis Club, a club for African-American players. Gibson's

family could not afford to join the group, so people in the Harlem community who recognized her potential raised money to pay for her membership and lessons.

As she improved, Gibson received another break: an African-American doctor, civil rights activist, and tennis fan named Hubert Eaton invited the teenager to come live with his family in South Carolina. As a result Gibson would get a good high school and college education, along with advanced tennis training.

Gibson soon was good enough to dominate the American Tennis Association (ATA). This was an organization of the top African-American tennis players. She won the ATA championship 10 times. But black players were not allowed to compete in events run by the U.S. Lawn Tennis Association (USLTA), the organization that included the best white players. By 1950, however, Gibson had become so good that the organization decided to allow her to play in the U.S. National Grass Court Championship, the country's most prestigious tennis tournament. She was the first black athlete, male or female, to compete in the tournament. Gibson won her first match, but lost in the second round.

=== Did You Know? ===

Before Althea Gibson, Ora Washington (1898–1971) was the most successful African-American woman tennis player. Washington won her first ATA singles title in 1929. She held the title for the next seven years, until 1936, then regained it once again in 1937. Washington's record of seven consecutive ATA singles titles would stand until 1947, when it was broken by Althea Gibson.

Over the next few years, Gibson struggled to keep up with the stronger competition of the USLTA. She also faced racism and discrimination. She was not allowed to play in some tournaments because she was black. She was not permitted to stay in hotels where the white players stayed. She was not invited to luncheons for the other top players.

By the mid-1950s, Gibson was at her peak as an athlete. In 1956, she became the first black athlete to win the French Open in Paris. She also

won the doubles title at Wimbledon, England, that year. The Wimbledon tennis tournament is one of the oldest and most prestigious tennis events in the world.

In 1957 Althea Gibson became the first African American to win the singles title at Wimbledon. Later that year, she became the first black player to win the U.S. Grass Court Championship. Gibson won both of these tournaments again in 1958.

Gibson retired from amateur tennis after the 1958 season. There was no professional women's tennis tour in those years, so she spent a few years playing exhibitions for money. She also took up golf, and in 1964 became the first African-American to play on the Ladies Professional Golf Association (LPGA) tour. She played for several years, but never won a tournament—her best finish was second.

Althea Gibson was a remarkable athlete. Her successes on the tennis court opened the way for later African-American stars like Arthur Ashe and, much later, the sisters Venus and Serena Williams. In 1971, Gibson was elected to the International Tennis Hall of Fame. She died on September 28, 2003, at age 76. After Gibson's death, tennis star Venus Williams said, "I am grateful to Althea Gibson for having the strength and courage to break through the racial barriers in tennis. . . . Her accomplishments set the stage for my success."

President Barack Obama and First Lady Michelle Obama stand in the background as former NBA star Bill Russell is introduced as a recipient of the Presidential Medal of Freedom during a 2011 White House event. This is the highest honor the U.S. government awards to civilians, and was given to commemorate Russell's work for African-American civil rights during the 1960s. Russell played 13 seasons during the 1950s and 1960s, helping the Boston Celtics to win 11 NBA championships during that time.

5

RACING AHEAD AND BREAKING RECORDS

The world watched as the Olympic sprinters raced for the gold. It was the final of the women's 4 x 100 meter relay at the 1960 Olympic Games. With the relay race three-quarters finished, the American women were in second place. They were two yards behind the leader as the last runner took the baton. This woman had once been told by doctors that she would never walk. Now the African-American speedster was running for gold.

SETTING OLYMPIC RECORDS

Wilma Rudolph had already won two gold medals in the 1960 Olympic Games. Could she win a third as the anchor of her relay team? She used her blazing speed and closed the gap. The "fastest woman in the world" kicked into high gear. The woman who had polio as a child made history when she crossed the finish line three yards ahead of the second-place German team. Wilma Rudolph became the first American woman to win three gold medals in a single Olympic Games.

Her victory on September 8, 1960, made headlines around the world. "The American runner Wilma Rudolph has confirmed her place in sporting history with a third Olympic gold medal in Rome," the British

Wilma Rudolph finishes first in a sprint event at New York's Madison Square Garden, 1961.

Broadcasting Corporation wrote. "Today's third gold in the relay event was thrilling to watch."

Back at home in the United States, the 20-year-old Rudolph became a heroine. But she was a heroine in a country divided by race and prejudice. In some states, African Americans couldn't eat in the same restaurants as whites. They couldn't stay in the same hotels. They couldn't use the same bathrooms. In the 1950s and 1960s, African Americans began protesting and demanding the same rights as white Americans. Their activities became known as the Civil Rights Movement.

Rudolph retired from track and field in 1962. During her athletic career, she won four Olympic medals and seven National Amateur Athletic

Union (AAU) titles. She was elected to the U.S. Olympic Hall of Fame in 1983. Rudolph died of brain cancer on November 12, 1994. She was 54.

WILT CHAMBERLAIN

Other black athletes soared to the top of their games during this same time period. In basketball, Wilt Chamberlain became a legend. The NBA champion was known as an unstoppable force on the hardwood in the 1960s and early 1970s. The league called the 7-foot-1-inch center the "most awesome offensive" player in the history of the game.

Wilton Norman Chamberlain grew up in Philadelphia. He was one of the top high school players in the country, scoring more than 2,220 points during his high school years.

Chamberlain became an All-American at the University of Kansas (KU). He scored 52 points in his first varsity game against Northwestern. Chamberlain left Kansas before his senior year and played a season with the Harlem Globetrotters.

In 1959, the NBA's Philadelphia Warriors drafted Chamberlain. During his rookie year, he averaged 37.9 points per game.

Wilt Chamberlain (1936–1999) in his Harlem Globetrotters uniform, 1959. He would dominate the NBA during the 1960s, leading the league in scoring seven times and in rebounding 11 times. Chamberlain won the NBA's Most Valuable Player award four times, and helped his teams win NBA titles in 1967 and 1972. He was so dominant that the NBA changed several rules to make the game harder for him.

RECORD-BREAKING CAREER

On March 2, 1962, Chamberlain sealed his place in basketball history. He scored 100 points in a game against the New York Knicks. That is more than any other NBA player has ever scored in a single game. The Warriors beat the Knicks 169-147 in that historic match-up. That season, Chamberlain averaged more than 50 points and 25 rebounds a game.

For most of his career, Chamberlain was a scoring machine. He led the NBA in scoring seven times, including six years in a row. He is the only NBA player to score over 4,000 points in one season. During his 14 years in the league, he scored a total of 31,419 points. Wilt "the Stilt" Chamberlain also grabbed 23,924 rebounds during his career. In all, Chamberlain set more than 40 league records.

Chamberlain retired after his 1973 season with the Los Angeles Lakers. He was elected to the Naismith Memorial Basketball Hall of Fame in 1978. Wilt Chamberlain died on October 22, 1999. He was 63.

LEW ALCINDOR (KAREEM ABDUL-JABBAR)

Another legendary player also started his reign on the court during the 1960s. Lew Alcindor ruled college basketball during his days at the University of California at Los Angeles (UCLA). The 7-foot-2-inch center averaged 26.4 points with the Bruins from 1966 to 1969. He was a master at dunking—so good that the NCAA worried Alcindor was unstoppable. In 1967, college basketball officials banned dunking. This became known as the "Alcindor Rule." The ruling didn't stop Alcindor. He mastered another shot, the sky hook, and used it to help the Bruins win three straight NCAA championships.

After graduating in 1969, Alcindor signed with the Milwaukee Bucks of the NBA. In each of his first three seasons, he scored more points than any other player in the league. He helped the Bucks win the NBA title in 1971. Afterward, he told reporters that a few years earlier, when he had become a Muslim, he had taken a new name, Kareem Abdul-Jabbar. He asked people to start calling him by the new name.

After the 1974-75 season, the Bucks traded Abdul-Jabbar to the Los Angeles Lakers. The center would help the Lakers become the best team in the NBA during the late 1970s and 1980s. Los Angeles won NBA titles in 1980, 1982, 1985, 1987, and 1988. During his 20-year career, Abdul-Jabbar was named the NBA's Most Valuable Player six times.

When Kareem Abdul-Jabbar retired after the 1988-89 season, he held many NBA records. He remains the league's all-time leading scorer with a total of 38,387 points. In 1995, Abdul-Jabbar was elected to the Naismith Memorial Basketball Hall of Fame.

ARTHUR ASHE

In the world of tennis, one black player took center court during the 1960s and 1970s. Arthur Ashe was born in Richmond, Virginia, in 1943 and started playing tennis as a boy. He won his first tournament when he was 12. In 1963 he received a scholarship to play tennis at UCLA. That same year, he became the first African American named to the U.S. Davis Cup team. (The Davis Cup is a prestigious international tennis competition.) Ashe would help the U.S. team win the Davis Cup tournament in 1968. That would turn out to be a great year for Ashe, as he won both the U.S. Amateur Championship and the first U.S. Open. This is one of the four most important annual events in tennis, known as the "Grand Slam" events.

Ashe became a professional tennis player in 1969, and in 1970 won his second Grand Slam title at the Australian Open. That year, he also took a public stand against discrimination in South Africa, where an official government policy called apartheid kept blacks and whites separate. The country wouldn't let the tennis legend play in the South African Open because he was black. Ashe wanted South Africa kicked out of the International Lawn Tennis Federation. In 1973, the South African government relented, and Ashe became the first black to play in its tournament.

During his career Ashe worked to help African Americans. He supported greater opportunities for black athletes in tennis and other sports. He raised millions of dollars to build tennis centers in urban neighborhoods,

so black kids could use them. He also raised money for the United Negro College Fund.

Ashe won 33 singles titles as a professional, including a third Grand Slam event, the 1975 Wimbledon title. In 1980, heart disease forced him to retire at age 36. He continued to work for the public good, becoming the national chairman of the American Heart Association and starting several charities. Ashe was inducted into the Tennis Hall of Fame in 1985.

In 1992, Ashe told the world that he had contracted the virus HIV, which causes AIDS, from blood he had received during surgery. Ashe died on February 6, 1993, at the age of 49.

BREAKING BABE'S RECORD

It should have been the highlight of Hank Aaron's career. The great baseball player had hit 714 home runs in his career, tying a record set by the legendary Babe Ruth. His first home run of the 1974 baseball season would set a new record. But the Atlanta Braves outfielder could not enjoy the moment. As he approached the Babe's home-run total, Aaron had begun to receive hate mail and death threats from people who didn't want a black ballplayer to hold one of the most prestigious records in baseball. "What was to have been his finest hour had become a monstrous ordeal," Ron Fimrite wrote in *Sports Illustrated*.

Aaron told the police about the threats, hired bodyguards, and warned his teammates not to sit next to him in the dugout. But he didn't stop playing. On April 8, 1974, he hit a high fastball over the leftfield fence at Atlanta Fulton County Stadium for his 715th home run. "I just thank God it's over," Aaron said after he crossed home plate.

Hank Aaron had been born in Mobile, Alabama, in 1934. As a teenager, he played in the Negro Leagues, helping the Indianapolis Clowns win the Negro League World Series in 1952. After this he signed a contract with the Milwaukee Braves. After two seasons with the Braves' minor-league teams, he reached the majors in 1954.

"Hammerin Hank" Aaron quickly became a star. He led the league in batting average twice, in home runs four times, and in runs batted in (RBIs)

Hank Aaron hits his record-breaking 715th home run on April 8, 1974. As he rounded the bases, his parents greeted him at home plate. "I just remember getting to the plate and my mother already being there," Aaron said. "To this day, I don't know how she got there so quickly. She gave me a tight hug. It was really a special moment."

four times. In 1957 he was named the National League's MVP for batting .322 with 44 home runs and 132 RBIs. That year he helped the Braves win the World Series, beating the New York Yankees. In 1958 Aaron led the Braves back to the series, but this time the Yankees won in seven games. During his 23-year career, Aaron was chosen for the all-star team 21 times.

Hank Aaron stayed with the Braves when the club moved from Milwaukee to Atlanta before the 1966 season. He led the league in home runs in 1966 (with 44) and 1967 (with 39). In 1969 his 44 homers helped Atlanta earn its first playoff spot, but the team was eliminated by the New York Mets. After the historic 1974 season, the Braves traded Hank Aaron back to Milwaukee, where a new team, the Brewers, had been started a few years earlier. When Hank Aaron retired two years later, he had hit more home runs (755) and driven in more RBIs (2,297) than any player in the history of major league baseball. At the time only Ty Cobb had more career hits than Aaron's 3,771.

Hank Aaron was elected to the Baseball Hall of Fame in 1982. Today, Major League Baseball gives the Hank Aaron Award each season to the best hitter in the National and American Leagues.

CASSIUS CLAY (MUHAMMAD ALI)

Cassius Clay might not have become a three-time World Heavyweight Champion if someone hadn't stolen his new bike when he was 12 years old. Clay, born in 1942, grew up in Louisville, Kentucky. When the bike was stolen, he told a local police officer he wanted to "whup" the thief. "You better learn to box first," responded the policeman, Joe Martin, who was also a boxing instructor.

Those words changed Clay's life. He started spending time in a local gym. He trained hard. Six weeks after the bike theft, Clay won his first match. He soon became a master in the ring. Clay won national championship titles in AAU and Golden Gloves competitions before he was 18.

During the 1960 Olympic Games in Rome, Clay won a gold medal in the light heavyweight division. After those games, Clay became a professional boxer. He won his first 19 fights, with 15 knockouts. This led to an opportunity to fight the world heavyweight champion, Sonny Liston, on February 25, 1964. Clay won the fight, and the title, in six rounds.

Clay's life outside the ring started making headlines, too. Clay joined an organization called the Nation of Islam and changed his name to Muhammad Ali. He began to speak about civil rights and criticized the U.S. government for being involved in the war in Vietnam. In 1967, when he was drafted into the U.S. Army,

Former heavyweight boxing champions Joe Frazier (1944–2011) and Muhammad Ali (b. 1942) joke at a 2002 event. In the early 1970s, the two boxers fought three of the greatest boxing matches of all time. Both are considered to be among the best heavyweight fighters ever.

Ali refused to serve. He was arrested, and his heavyweight title was taken away. He was not allowed to fight again for three years.

By 1970, Ali was back in the ring. He fought notable fights against Joe Frazier and Ken Norton to set up a showdown with George Foreman, who had won the title from Frazier in 1973. Most people expected Foreman to win their fight, which was held in Zaire, Africa, on October 30, 1974. However, Ali knocked Foreman out to reclaim the world heavyweight title.

In 1975, Ali fought Joe Frazier for a third time. This fight between two great heavyweights is considered one of the most dramatic fights in history. Ali won in the 15th round.

Ali lost the heavyweight title to Leon Spinks in 1978, but beat Spinks in a rematch six months later. This made him the first boxer to win the world heavyweight title three times. He retired as champion in 1979, although he later fought and lost a couple of bouts as part of a comeback attempt. During his career, Ali won 56 times, 37 by knockout, and lost five. In 1998, the boxing magazine *Ring* named Ali the greatest heavyweight of all time.

Muhammad Ali's political activism during the 1960s made him a cultural icon and a hero to millions people, both black and white. The legendary boxer who once claimed to "float like a butterfly, sting like a bee" is now battling Parkinson's disease. This condition causes muscle tremors and slurred speech. Ali still helps several charities, and raises money for the Muhammad Ali Parkinson Center in Phoenix, Arizona.

BLACK PLAYERS IN GOLF

Golf is a sport that has historically been dominated by white players. Blacks were not permitted to play in events held by the Professional Golfers Association (PGA) until 1961. That year, Charlie Sifford (b. 1922) became the first black golfer on the PGA Tour. During his career Sifford won two tournaments.

Another pioneering African American golfer was Lee Elder (b. 1934), who in 1975 became the first black to play in the prestigious Masters Tournament in Augusta, Georgia. The Masters is one of golf's four most

Sisters Venus and Serena Williams are the most successful African-American tennis players. They have won a total of 20 Grand Slam singles titles, as well as dozens of other events.

prestigious annual events (these are known as the "majors"). It is held at an exclusive country club that at the time did not allow blacks to be members. Elder did not play particularly well, but his appearance marked another step forward for black athletes in golf. During his career, Elder won four PGA Tour events.

In the 1980s, Calvin Peete (b. 1943) was one of the most successful golfers on the PGA Tour, winning 12 times. In 1984 he became the first African American to win the Vardon Trophy for lowest scoring average.

Their achievements opened the way for Tiger Woods (b. 1975), who was the first black golfer to win the U.S. Amateur title. He won the title three times, then joined the PGA Tour in 1996. The next year, Woods won the Master's Tournament. He was the youngest winner ever and broke the record for the lowest score. Over the next 15 years, Tiger dominated the PGA Tour like no player ever had. To date he has won more than 70 PGA Tour events. His 14 victories in major tournaments are second only to Jack Nicklaus's 18 majors—a record that Woods has been aiming to break since he was young. Tiger Woods is one of the greatest golfers ever to play the game.

* * *

By the 1980s, the successes of pioneering African-American athletes had opened the way for greater participation by blacks in mainstream sports. Today, 78 percent of NBA players and 67 percent of NFL players are black. In professional baseball, about 10 percent of the players are

Shani Davis competes at the World Sprint Speed Skating Championship in Russia.

African Americans. Blacks are also getting more opportunities as head coaches and team executives. In the 2012 NFL season, there were seven black head coaches, the most in the league's history.

African-American athletes have made inroads into other sports as well. In 2002, Vonetta Flowers became the first black person to win a medal at the Winter Olympics, winning gold as part of a two-person bobsled team. At the 2006 Winter Olympics, speedskater Shani Davis became the first black to win individual medals at the winter games. He won gold in the 1000 meter race and silver in the 1500 meter race. He repeated these accomplishments at the 2010 Winter Olympics.

Today, African-American athletes are judged by their talent, not the color of their skin.

CHAPTER NOTES

p. 10: "We believe that . . ." Bob Kendrick, quoted in Robert Falkoff, "Negro League Legacy." http://mlb.mlb.com/mlb/history/mlb_negro_leagues_story.jsp?story=museum

p. 10: "We have already got rid . . ." Lauren R. Harrison, "Exhibit Honors a Tested Pride, Passion," *Chicago Tribune* (September 2, 2010). http://articles.chicagotribune.com/2010-09-02/entertainment/ct-play-0902-quotes-baseball-exhibit-20100902_1_exhibit-honors-african-american-baseball-experience-jackie-s-gift

p. 10: "The taunts angered him . . ." interview with Rachel Robinson, Scholastic.com (February 11, 1998). http://www2.scholastic.com/browse/article.jsp?id=4808

p. 11: "Of course, I can't begin . . ." "Montreal Signs Negro Shortstop," *New York Times*, October 23, 1945.

p. 12: "I was nervous in the first..." "Double By Reiser Beats Boston," *New York Times*, April 16, 1947.

p. 12: "[Robinson] had all the attributes . . ." Bob Kendrick, quoted in Falkoff, "Negro League Legacy."

p. 12: "[Reese] stared into the Cincinnati dugout . . ." Hal Bodley, "Robinson Drew Praise from Many Corners," *USA Today* (April 13, 2007). http://www.usatoday.com/sports/baseball/columnist/bodley/2007-04-13-bodley-remembering-robinson_N.htm

p. 16: "American sports are filled . . ." Melvin R. Sylvester, "African Americans in the Sports Arena," B. Davis Schwartz Memorial Library, C.W. Post Campus of Long Island University, 1997. (link: http://www2.liu.edu/cwis/cwp/library/aaitsa.htm#plancke)

p. 25: "Rube knew that if Negroes . . ." Kadir Nelson, *We Are the Ship: The Story of Negro League Baseball,* (New York: Jump at the Sun/Hyperion Books For Children, 2008), p. 9.

p. 28: After you strike three . . ." Mamie "Peanut" Johnson, quoted in Scott Simon, "Mamie 'Peanut' Johnson, Pitching Pioneer," National Public Radio (February 18, 2003). http://www.npr.org/templates/story/story.php?storyId=1164167

p. 32:   "When I came back . . ." Larry Schwartz, "Owens Pierced a Myth," ESPN.com (2007). http://espn.go.com/sportscentury/features/00016393.html

p. 38:   "Jim Brown was a superb . . ." Pro Football Hall of Fame, "Jim Brown." http://www.profootballhof.com/hof/member.aspx?PLAYER_ID=33

p. 43:   "I am grateful to Althea Gibson . . ." Venus Williams, quoted in "First Black Tennis Player Althea Gibson Dies in East Orange, NJ, at 76," *Jet* (October 13, 2003).

p. 45:   "The American runner Wilma Rudolph . . ." "Rudolph takes third Olympic Gold," British Broadcasting Corp., September 11, 1960. http://news.bbc.co.uk/onthisday/hi/dates/stories/september/11/newsid_3554000/3554568.stm.

p. 50:   "What was to have been . . ." Ron Fimrite, A Look Back at Aaron's Ordeal," *Sports Illustrated* (September 19, 1994). http://sportsillustrated.cnn.com/baseball/mlb/features/1999/aaron/20years/

p. 50:   "I just thank God it's over," Ron Fimrite, "End of the Glorious Ordeal," *Sports Illustrated* (April 15, 1974). http://sportsillustrated.cnn.com/baseball/mlb/features/1999/aaron/aaron_story/)

p. 51:   "I just remember getting to the plate . . ." Mark Bowman, "Q&A with Home Run King Hank Aaron," MLB.com (May 22, 2007). http://atlanta.braves.mlb.com/news/article.jsp?ymd=20070507&content_id=1950983&vkey=news_mlb&fext=.jsp&c_id=mlb

p. 52:   "You better learn to box first," Gregory Allen Howard, "The Boxer, The Official Site of Muhammad Ali." http://www.ali.com/legend_boxer_main.php

CHRONOLOGY

1865	The Thirteenth Amendment to the U.S. Constitution officially ends slavery in the United States.
1887	Professional baseball teams impose a "gentleman's agreement" to stop allowing blacks to play.
1891	James A. Naismith invents the game of basketball.
1902	Joe Gans, a lightweight fighter from Baltimore, becomes the first African American to win a world boxing championship.
1920	The Negro National League is formed.
1929	The Great Depression starts. Millions of people lose their money, jobs, and homes.
1936	Jesse Owens wins four gold medals at the Olympic Games in Berlin.
1937	Joe Louis becomes the second black boxer to win the World Heavyweight title.
1947	On April 15, Jackie Robinson breaks the color barrier in baseball when he plays his first game with the Brooklyn Dodgers.
1960	Wilma Rudolph wins three gold medals at the Olympic Games in Rome.
1962	Wilt Chamberlain sets an NBA record by scoring 100 points in a single game.
1975	Arthur Ashe wins the singles title at Wimbledon, and is ranked as the number one tennis player in the world.
1974	Hank Aaron hits his 715th home run, breaking Babe Ruth's record.
1997	Tiger Woods becomes the first African-American golfer to win a major tournament, the Masters.
2006	Speed skater Shani Davis becomes the first African American to win an individual medal in a Winter Olympics.
2007	For the first time in NFL history, the coaches for both teams in the Super Bowl (Tony Dungy of the Indianapolis Colts and Lovie Smith of the Chicago Bears) are black.

GLOSSARY

barnstorm—a term for traveling around the country to perform in sporting events. This was common among baseball, basketball, and football clubs in the first half of the 20th century.

electrifying—exciting.

Grand Slam—a term for the four major tennis tournaments held each year. They include the Australian Open, the French Open, Wimbledon, and the U.S. Open.

gridiron—a football field.

legendary—famous.

majors—nickname for the four most important golf tournaments held each year. The majors include the Masters Tournament, the U.S. Open, the British Open, and the PGA Championship.

mock—to tease or make fun of someone.

prejudice—hatred, fear, or mistrust of a person or groups of people.

rampage—to move about wildly.

revere—to treat someone with great respect.

scrimmage—a practice game.

segregate—to separate people or groups of people based on their race or other characteristics.

squelched—to silence something.

taunt—to tease someone in a hurtful way.

FURTHER READING

Buckley, James, et al., *50 Years of American Sports: A Decade-by-Decade History*. New York: World Almanac, 2010.

Fleder, Rob. *The Basketball Book*. New York: Time, 2007.

Gutman, Bill. *Venus & Serena: the Grand Slam Williams Sisters*. New York: Scholastic, 2001.

Nelson, Kadir. *We Are the Ship: the Story of Negro League Baseball*. New York: Jump at the Sun/Hyperion for Children, 2008.

Porter, David L. *African-American Sports Greats: A Biographical Dictionary*. Westport, Conn.: Greenwood Press,1995.

INTERNET RESOURCES

http://www.sikids.com/

This is the Web site for *Sports Illustrated for Kids*. It is a kid-friendly version of the magazine that includes information about sports, teams, and star players.

http://www.olympic.org/en/

This is the official Web site for the Olympic Games. It includes information about past Olympics, as well as the athletes who competed in them. It also has information about upcoming Olympic Games.

http://memory.loc.gov/ammem/collections/robinson/jr1860s.html

The Library of Congress created this special online exhibit called "Baseball, the Color Line, and Jackie Robinson."

http://www.nlbpa.com/index.html

This is the Web site for the Negro League Baseball Players Association. It includes information about the players and teams in the Negro Leagues.

INDEX

Numbers in **bold italics** refer to captions.

CONTRIBUTORS

JAMES NASIUM has written for the sports pages of several newspapers. This is his first book.

Senior Consulting Editor **DR. MARC LAMONT HILL** is one of the leading hip-hop generation intellectuals in the country. Dr. Hill has lectured widely and provides regular commentary for media outlets like NPR, the *Washington Post*, *Essence Magazine*, the *New York Times*, CNN, MSNBC, and *The O'Reilly Factor*. He is the host of the nationally syndicated television show *Our World With Black Enterprise*. Dr. Hill is a columnist and editor-at-large for the *Philadelphia Daily News*. His books include the award-winning *Beats, Rhymes, and Classroom Life: Hip-Hop Pedagogy and the Politics of Identity* (2009).

Since 2009 Dr. Hill has been on the faculty of Columbia University as Associate Professor of Education at Teachers College. He holds an affiliated faculty appointment in African American Studies at the Institute for Research in African American Studies at Columbia University.

Since his days as a youth in Philadelphia, Dr. Hill has been a social justice activist and organizer. He is a founding board member of My5th, a non-profit organization devoted to educating youth about their legal rights and responsibilities. He is also a board member and organizer of the Philadelphia Student Union. Dr. Hill also works closely with the ACLU Drug Reform Project, focusing on drug informant policy. In addition to his political work, Dr. Hill continues to work directly with African American and Latino youth.

In 2005, *Ebony* named Dr. Hill one of America's 100 most influential Black leaders. The magazine had previously named him one of America's top 30 Black leaders under 30 years old.